Sadness & Beauty

Sadness & Beauty

A Collection of Poetry

Kelly De Guia

Library of Congress Control Number:		2019908876
ISBN:	Hardcover	978-1-7960-0450-2
	Softcover	978-1-7960-0449-6
	eBook	978-1-7960-0448-9

To order additional copies of this book, contact:
Xlibris
1-800-455-039
www.Xlibris.com.au
Orders@Xlibris.com.au
799188

CONTENTS

For life is both the mountains and the valleys.
The good and the bad; we cannot have one without the other.
We need both to truly understanding living.

To the people behind the words, thank you for the love & pain.

THE HATE & LOVE OF WRITTEN WORDS

'I have hated the words and I have loved them,
and I hope I have made them proud'
-Marcus Zusak 'The Book Thief'

I F THERE IS one line or description of how I feel about writing and how I feel about poetry, it would be the last line in the Book Thief. It is the perfect summary of my experience in writing, a description that outlines why I write or more so why I continue to write poetry. You see words have, in moments been my friend and my enemy, they have been the weapon of affliction and also my source of hope. Whether it has been my own words or words written by other, they have provided the ability to feel a shared connection and have expressed moments of suppressed emotions. Written Words have been my voice in times of self-failure, during the moments where I could not speak truth, anger or heartbreak. Words were magic when pen touched paper and suppressed truth came out, my tool of communication for all things on the basis of love, life and loss. All at the same time of being one of the big frustrations I deal with; the stubbornness of betrayed, convicted moment by the very words I have written and the words I have read. This collection, Sadness and Beauty, brings light to the beginning of my writing journey that started as an outlet of expression through the musings of journal thoughts. My coping mechanism called Carey.

A daily schedule that was named after my high school. Carey was not a place of peace, but the place where I was introduced to my love or more so my unknown need of writing. Carey was and is still a place of memory. It is the only place where I can combine emotions and memories of past with present reality and somewhat feel like an opened time capsule. It goes beyond the place and the name. Carey is the familiar yet different pathways, hidden laneways and buildings that

I can walk around and recall specific moments as if they are dancing around me, like a movie reel of the best and worst years of my youthful life. Carey the school and the writing tool allowed me to recall the long hours and access emotion of both joy, naivety and pain felt in the past and now.

The importance of Carey was just like writing, it was not just something for the past, it is a mixture of all three (past, present and future). Both become the tool to hold on to past memories, laugh at the adventures of today and look at the list of hopes and dreams set for the future. Carey is a place where I when I am back amongst the scenery, can for a moment stand and peer into the small office, through the brown stained-glass door and audibly hear the conversation with the counsellor and the simple idea and the words that will forever haunt me, *'Kelly Just write, write all that you cannot say, not for anyone to read, but for yourself, for your future, for you now in the moment and for the moments in your past you still don't understand, let the words tell your story'.*

Words become my story, it became the outlook to write about hidden truths and emotions that reflect and bring light to the range of moments from the struggle of life trials, admirable sadness in growing up and changing, laughter and joy felt in badly worded jokes and highlights of high school puppy love and naïve crushes. Carey was the starting line of writing through it, I gained the ability to express my emotions, complicated thoughts all through words. It was the means for expressing the moments I loved and wanted to cherish but represented the hanger and confusion of memories where at the time, words were stuck or kept back. My written words, and this collection have and still do tell my story of the mountains and valleys.

For to hate and to love words, brought about the idea for Sadness and Beauty. It was only recently at the end of 2018 that I started too truly appreciate both sides of life, the good and the bad. The beauty in the moments when we are in love, happy, when life just feels like we are on the top of the mountains. Has also brought about the appreciation in the hardship and sense of learning experienced in the valleys when we are aching confused, lost and hurt. Maybe not in the exact minute we experience such hurdles but in the moments of reflection, looking back and laughing we somehow realize how right the words we hated actually saved us and grudgingly helped us. 'Sadness and Beauty' which actually was another person's perspective of me became the summary to the balance beam of life. The revelation that experiencing both the mountain tops and valleys are essential to truly living out life and enjoy the ride.

That's why I continue to write. Writing became more then just a tool, it became my memory, my story of life. It is what I will leave behind when I one day move on. For the past decade of my life I have been writing for myself, about the aspects of love, life and faith. My trinity of life. I continue to write to save myself from the chaos and clutter of thoughts. For words have at times just flowed through and at times words are the fragmented sentences of inner stress. Writing overall has always been a lesson to life. I write to learn more about my situation, my true feelings and the lessons and experiences I still and will continue to face. A Constant lesson I may not really truly grasp. Poetry also has taught me the lesson of patience; that sometimes patience is needed in life and in writing. Everything is not made instant. Through poetry I have learnt that at times it may take months to find the words to relay the message of the moment and sometimes words will feel so natural and are just naturally waiting to burst out. I am constantly being reminded that sometimes simplicity is the key; there is no need for big words, but to just write simple and the beauty will come out.

I write for that beauty in words, something that cannot be found elsewhere. It is the simple, uncomplicated feeling that a few words in a line can make or break a moment. There is a magic in the ability that reading written words has, where I can look back and read the poetry of certain moments on the heartache of love, revelations of life chapters, the joy and happiness in moments of true laughter and infatuations, and automatically be reconnected to the emotion of the past. Like every line read brings about the distant memories to mingle with the realm of today, whether it be grief, anger, love or heartache there truly is this catharsis of sharing the emotion sometimes known and sometimes suppressed. Where there is an unspoken acknowledgement that sometimes thoughts and feelings are actually better just written down then said out loud.

I write to hopefully leave behind a part of my story. Shakespeare once said life is a tapestry all woven into one. Imagine everyone had a story chapter, what a grand book, but the reality is that not every chapter would be interesting. I just hope to be able to leave a glimpse into my journey and to one day have my words be the evidence to all that I was capable of in life. When I realized that life was the mixture of the beauty and the sadness, the alert went off that I don't write now just for myself. That what started out as the tool to express the emotion, became a reflection into my real self. Sadness and beauty this collection is the start of that. It is the opportunity to take hold of the moments of bliss and infatuation and not fear acknowledging the moments of tears and sorrow and be okay in that. For **beauty** lets us grow and **sadness**, despite hurting like hell, will shape and strengthen an individual. To me that the quintessence of life; the good and the bad. The book thief ended with the best description for the goal of writing, I hope I have made the words proud, I have felt the beauty and the sadness in written works and in my own words, but all I can do is continue to hope that the I have made the words proud.

William Carey Christian School 'Carey'

PART I

Love

*'The greatest thing one will ever learn is to
just love and be loved in return'*
– Nat King Cole

I BELIEVE THAT LOVE is something we never truly master. Love is something that will be a lifelong lesson, that does not mean we will never experience love, but that love will always change and grow with age. Our interest and attractions won't always be the same. Just look at what you are interested now and compare it to what you were interested in when you were 10 even 26 or 18, they were all different. But what we were attracted to during those years, were all the things we loved, it does not mean now we love them less or more but that we changed in love. I am no expert on the matter of love in fact I am a learner of life and all things love, where others are great professors, even teachers in the chapters of love, I am still beginning the journey; still learning and experiencing things for the first time. I have had my share of experiences and the times where I've questioned if love was truly felt, not to take away from the moments but more so a realization that times that I once perceived as love, are actually in hindsight moments of admiration. They were moments where love was everything it shouldn't be. Love was vain, love was selfish, love was childish. Despite the constant question of, was it love or was it just life seen through rose colored glasses; there's a confidence that what I experienced were the characteristics of love. From the infatuation to the ache of letting go, there were aspects of love felt. Even if it was the not the right love, even when it was a selfish or neutral love, the essence of love was present.

So, what is love? Well, in my opinion, love is the moments where time stood still, and warmth enveloped my world. The moments where laughter filled the bedroom walls and every date was another step forward in learning, but love was felt at the darker times. Love was present in the moments my heart hurt, and broken promises were witness to the failure of hollow words. Its love in the moments I saw the offence I caused through own confessions and unnecessary lies, moments where self – interest took over. Despite the greatest joy or the worst ache, love is that mixture of the uncontrolled tears and days under covers. The moments when no words were needed, attraction screaming through touch and loved up looks. For it does not matter where we find ourselves at or at what age we are, if it's not through romance, it may be friendship or kinship, or the admiration, but whenever we go through and there is clearly a moment of remembrance, rest assure that love was present in all. That love will be stitched into the fabric of the memories, past present and future.

I look back and I have learnt that everyone goes through their own journey in love, that not one persons story will ever be the same. Every time we're greeted with the adventure of love it will always come about differently. Some endings we will remember for the heartache, some we will be glad the end has come (the argument better late than never), some we will remember for the outpour of love and then there are the few that goodbye won't ever happen life just altered differently. I know personally there have been many times I have been infatuated and hit hard with the love bug, but only a few times in my life have I truly been in love or experienced a whirlwind of romance. Each person, despite what role or relationship they were a part of helped me grow in life and helped me come to know and understand worth. They all were different, all made me wonder and do some crazy things.

Everyone has their own attraction, their own interaction with the notion of love, what you would count as love will not be the same for any other, not even your own partner. When we are five, love was just family, until playground crushes meant the world. Playground crushes become teenagers and pass around notes of confessions and brave questions, the moments where the person of our dreams takes over most of our life, it's also the time where most start to question love, or even at times mix lust for love. There are the special few, the ones that go from friendship to romance or romance to lifelong friends, where lines are blurred and its better for some time to continue that way. Was one better than the other? No because during that season during that time of life, that is what I was looking for, that is what I was attracted to. \

There will be the moments where love is like the many books we read, all one genre but never the same story, similar concepts and storylines but the characters and the realms bring about the difference in all that we want and need. A old blockbuster, A love story is famous for the tagline of the movie, it states, 'love means never having to say you're sorry'; and for such a long time I thought well, that's not right if I am wrong or if I have been hurt, I expect to apologize and hope to hear the words **I'm sorry**. It was not until my final year of university where I was introduced to love and the seriousness of actions that I was reunited with an old friend, my first love. The one who I learnt too late the consequences of our actions when it comes to love and fighting. It was a reunion unexpected, but may it be fate, or just our dear friend once again meddling but we had a conversation and we were remembering this movie, a favorite of both of ours.

He told me his perception of the quote. *'To never say I'm sorry, is not about the arguments and who was wrong or right, because then we both would have died. No, that movie, that line it's about not being guilty in loving someone, in doing everything you can to be with that person. It's never having to say sorry for the sacrifices or the things we let go of to be with the one we love., Kelly never having to say you're sorry is not to be prideful, but it's because of love that we change and make these decisions.'*

We reunited, after a year of parting, there was regret and there were unanswered questions to our journey together. You see through him I learnt love, and because of him I also experienced heartache; we used to always say, I'm sorry, more times than we actually needed. Looking back now, we realized, even though there was hurt and pain it was a necessity. We needed that chapter to continue to grow, we needed that to continue to learn. Like I said, Love is a lesson for life, one we will always never get perfect but what we can do is to learn to just love and **(oh God hope)** to be loved in return. F Scott Fitzgerald once famously said; *'there are all kinds of love in this world, but never the same love twice'.*

That is the essence of my experiences and my perspective of love. I am not saying that my perspective is the right kind, like I said I am no expert but what I have experience is that I can or have had the chance to love people in different ways and in different stages of my life. One gave to me what the other could not and one helped me become where I am now. I think essentially that is the beauty in the notion of love. The fact that when it comes to love, and relationships we are a part of they will never be the same, for the love I have for my family is not the same love I have for my friends, the love I have for my siblings is not the same that I have for my boyfriend or my ex boyfriends, but I love and have loved them all, and I have also felt the love both in the pain and in joy. Love will never be clear, never be so black and white, it will always be different. If anything Love will be exactly what we wanted at the moment, maybe looking back we find ourselves foolish for holding on when it was obvious to let go or laughing at what our expectations of love was when it came along and how it looked but that, that is the power of love.

And yet there is the love of oneself, confidence in who I am and hope in all I could be. That is the aspect of this section of love, I have been hurt and I have hurt others but what I do know is that every goodbye that made me cry and every hello that made me blush allowed the words to flow. Some took months after for the words to express the reality of the situation and others where always just free flowing. Love is the mixture of the kisses and the misses, the infatuation and the anger. The moments of silent sheepish glances, and city night adventures but it is also of heartache and empty boxes of tissue. Love is something I have hated writing about, and at the same time it is also something I cherish. The ability to write and describe the warm feeling or butterflies when I am met with someone new or to open up old journals and read the feelings of infatuation and romance.

The ability to recall moments from years or months ago. It was only through writing that I have been able to share suppressed affection perfectly through words. There have been many times when words fail me in the minute of reality so having the words on paper helps reassure decisions or doubts of what ifs. It has been through the writings during breakups and the romance that I have been able to understand more of who I am and what I deserve. Writing has expressed my gratitude and immortalized favorite memories where scenes were not captured but the words described the feeling and the thoughts of the day. I have continued to learn about love and worth through the ramblings of my written thoughts.

So, what is love? Well truthfully, I question that statement. Can one truly answer that so simple? I think that what I define as love now as a twenty-five-year-old, is not the same definition I would have had when I was three, fifteen or even when I am forty because love changes and our perspective of love changes.

The following poems in this section show the adventures and misadventures of my relationships, not all written when I was in them some written about crushes or mutual understandings, some written about the heartache of my first love and boyfriends who have impacted me. Some unwritten letters, and hidden thoughts, truth I was confronted with but didn't want to accept, until a few years later. Love is a multifaceted thing but like I sad earlier love is a lesson, I am still learning about love, about loving myself, and about trying to understand my wants and needs for now, for my future and for my past self who went through the heartache and the pain but also who was smart enough to just have fun when needed. Some loves were childish, somewhere just to pass the time, one was and still is a mystery a question I am still trying to answer. But all have taught me all have molded me.

All experiences are my teaching lessons. I guess that's the lesson we learn right, like the lyrics to the song, the great lesson is **TO LOVE AND TO BE LOVED IN RETURN**. Did I love more at times, well yes, did I love less and take the moment for granted definitely. No. None have ever been perfect and maybe in a year or in a few months, I will be able to understand more about love, because I have loved them all, I have felt attraction and admiration but there is always a difference of loving someone and being in love with someone. At the end of the day the people behind the poems, the ones the words were written for, they have all been impactful, I remember and cherish each memory. The painful ones and the ones that still today bring a comfort and warmth when I re-read the memories and the emotion, I felt for them then, for they were what I wanted, everything I thought I deserved I don't regret how any ended. There are still what ifs? But not every goodbye is sad, not every goodbye was the end. So, what is love well all I can say are what I learnt through my experiences what I wrote through the poems.

LOVE

THE KISSES & THE MISSES

What is love? Is it a feeling?
Is it a person? Is it a favorite memory?
Love is maybe not just one thing, maybe it's all three.
I see love when tired parents stay up all
night with a sick child and still work the next morning.
lack of sleep, guilt in heading off to make a living.
It's the blanket forts and nerf battles of sibling laughter
around the house. Love is the kisses and the tight
embraces that fill the house night and day.
It's in the way moms and dads are last to slumber, while the
chaos of their child's playful minds are put to rest.
I see love in the humbleness of saying sorry, breaking
the silence that filled the house for days. No longer wanting
distance when the one we cherish is at arm's length.
It's the moment of saying 'I forgive you', and 'I still love you'.
Letting someone know they're not bound by past mistakes.
Love is the act of service, knowing they need it more then you.
Its putting someone first above one's self and saying hey 'I'll do
It again, everyday just for you'.
You see I have learnt, and am continuing to learn
that love is many things, it's not just simply a person,
a feeling or our favorite memory. It's the words I love you,
I am here, I am staying, thank you and I'm sorry.
It's the looks we give to the ones who make us smile,
those moments, when no words are needed
but the sparkle in their eyes know how appreciated one can be.
Love is a splendid thing; love is something we cannot truly
explain, as corny as it seems, love is something we truly
have to act and feel.

I cannot say there are many things,
I have loved so far in life,
there are several I've admired,
infatuated, even lust over.
To say I have loved, many times I'm still unsure.
There are memories and moments
I treasure so dearly
that still stirs within my inner core.
I have respected the early morning sun rays
playing with the shadows of the night before.
I have prized the first sip of black coffee,
in the morning followed by a nice warm shower.
I have gleamed at the connection felt
in reading other people's words.
Laughing at the stories told,
feeling the written joy, as if it was my own.
I have chuckled at the random dancing
when my favorite song plays out loud,
whether it be on the wooden floor
or the inside of my bedroom walls.
I have admired the greenery surrounding
when I take that afternoon stroll,
the smell of fresh mowed grass,
a moment known that spring has sprung.
I have cherished the moments of long car rides
from day or night adventures,
surrounded by my closest ones
where silence is all that's needed.
No words, no music, just the story of
the shadows dancing to our sides.
I passionately recall moments
where he kissed me, even against the wall.

When the mixture of lust and love had filled the air.
I long for driven conversations of reality and war,
to hear generations, differ in views and policy law.
But respect around the table,
with open ears and minds to all.
I love these small moments, the ones we pass by quickly,
for I may not have a favorite still unsure on moments of true love,
but it is known for certain that love was felt in all the seconds spent.

One day I'll find him, the one my soul will love.
The one there'll be no doubt, when we say the words 'I Do'.
But before that day will come,
there is one I need to learn to love.
A person who needs to know they're okay
and exactly where they're needed.
She is the girl who looks at the mirror,
just to turn away so suddenly,
ashamed at who is looking back.
unsure what others see when they're looking at her daily.
She is the girl who second guesses,
every good that comes her way.
Questions if it's really hers
just waiting for the ache to start.
Already expecting the joy to end.
She is the girl who reads the countless stories
of romance and love affairs,
hoping it may one day be her reality.
The tales of night activities and weekend
adventures is what she dreams,
yet thoughts and doubts of who would want her,
just laugh in her face.
She is the girl, who's scared of committing,
unable to take another pain.
She questions why no ones left,
believe she's the reason why.
So, before I say I love you and before I say I do,
I need to break away the wall.
I need to pick the little girl and cradle her some more.
I need to slay the dragons of her mind and wish it all away.
I need to tell her daily, 'you're loved', just look around.
I need to tell young Kelly; 'it's okay, go love yourself'.

And if there's no tomorrow, and all we have is today,
the present moment, I am glad that I have you,
that you're known to my soul.
You're like a sweet summers breeze
or the crispness on a winter day.
You're the beauty one notices only
in the falling leaves of May.
So, I will hold on. I will hold on for the luck of life.
I will embrace all that comes my way,
with you here by my side from you I cannot hide,
I can no longer fight it. But please just sit and listen.
Let me tell you a story of how
heartache and pain, saw the glitter
amidst the stormy day.
How sunlight spilt and made the
end a new beginning.
A story of love and lost,
the best of both worlds.
To tell you the tale,
a battle of darkness and light
inside and out, trying to keep it all at bay.
A story of no happy ending, but no ending at all.
I'll write it all down, it's easier that way.
For sometimes words spoken are not enough.
Sometimes the gaps of silence,
say more than the words that follow.
You see the familiarity you carry is a calming thought.
I knew the minute I met you, you'll be something new.
I am reminded of you daily through
the simple things I see.
It's in the chuckle of a laugh,
the silence in an arty observation.
Reminded in the couple sat in front and the look they share.
I feel the butterflies and think when you
look at me that way.

KELLY DE GUIA

It's the randomness of life
I remember how you changed me
Unknowingly and stubbornly changed life's perspective.
That's the blessing and the curse
you bring wherever you will go.
For despite the sweetness that you hold,
you still are the closed eyelid,
looking up at a sunny spring day.

To the boy who taught me love,
you were the one who sat and laughed at life.
The end of many, but you were just a lesson.
Looking back, we're the support we both
without admitting needed.

Moments in the cramped and dusty room,
just writing on the floor, mixed laughter and silenced pain
When words failed to say move on to life's next stage.
Unsure where to go, we found a comfort in each
other aching. Do you remember the hopes we
shared for joint future goals?

You taught me love and you taught me hurt.
not in broken promises but in life letting go.
We knew goodbye was coming,
we had to go our separate ways,
no words needed when time ticked by,
just tightness and then emptiness.
You were the first encounter with love.
The moment of a loved-up bubble, of scribbled notes and
holding hands. For when I think of love at the young age,
Love has brown hair, and the mix smell of lynx cans and paint.

As life goes on, love now has changed. No longer
the smell of paint and laughter, love was now desire.
To the boy, who broke my heart, as you broke yours.
I'm sorry and I'm grateful, now love came back no longer
Childish with the kid like manner. Love now strong and tall,
love now dark blond, metal framed glasses and the sweet
scent of old spice and lemonade.

Love now liked politics and laughed at random articles.
Love brought about new experiences. Love brought about fights.
Where to go, just say no, love was what I wanted but life was saying

to let go. The day we met democracy made us laugh.
The day I said enough, democracy was the awkward silence.
My first experience with make the most of the time we have.
I loved too late for you were now a state away.
Now you're happy, now your married. Now you're everything you dreamt.
We taught each other love, and our very first heartache.

Years had passed and loved hid itself away.
Masked through drunken nights and strangers in the dark.
Until the day love had reappeared.
Not in all the glitz and glamour, no love was just the simplest hello.
The sunshine peeking amidst the stormy days.
love appeared and said stop trying, you're okay.
When I think back to the way love appeared, the
random stages of my life. Love was never just a person
but love was the moment of memory in the situation that occurred.
Love is always changing, but love is always there.
For love will say hello and one day love will say let's go home.
Love now many faces, Love is always there.

In a tunnel of youth and childhood memories
we sat and laughed with talk of the future,
excitement for what's to come.
Paused and smiled at the adventures of today.
Glad to be in each other's embrace.
Where playful looks and soft touches
made the night sky and city lights seem so bright.
the thought of winter now a pleasant surprise.
The show of lights and sounds, a festival of ideas.
Crowded places, but here is where I focused on
Everything else just blurred phases passing by.
Sydney alive like the main on the opera stage.
it's the moment just sitting or walking hand in hand
the thought appears, 'there's still hope in the craziness of life'.
Evidence in the world around.

You look at me and I can't help but smile.
Like how crazy it is to be high on life to
let life cares and struggles fade into the ground.
For just one night, I'm glad I have you in my life.
Whatever capacity, I know you're there even right here.
Just one night, I'm reminded I'm cared for and that's alright.

I no longer care for the idea of small talk
Let us get passed the ordinary 'hi, how are you?'
I no longer want to talk about the Netflix show or
The final of the game we both don't really care.
Tell me your curiosity, talk about your passion
Let me in to the things that scare and frighten you.
It's not that I don't want to hear about your goofy friends and
the prank they saw through another viral video.
I'm more interested in the time you felt alive.
Open about the time you messed up. When you felt
like a fool for trusting yet another person to fail you.
Teach me of the lesson learnt through your hardest times.
I long to hear your inspiration, your motivation, your doubts.
All stupid fears and life worries, on everything from work to future goals.
Profess your humanity, cause boy I no longer want
The small talk conversations.
Cliché as it seems, time we don't really have.
we don't know how long till we say that final goodbye.
I want to love you and I want to know you,
Under the sheets or in the bus, I want to show you all.
So, stop all bullshit and show me who you are.
No masks, no hidden fears, let us be so vulnerable,
exposed at each other's side.
Talk about how you felt the moment you said hello,
or the moment your heart broke for the first time.
Tell me the difference between I love you and I like you.
Your darkest sorrow and the moments of pure joy,
I want to hear the stories of laughter that turned to tears
or tears that turned into laughter. I want to hear when you
called your mom last and laughed with your father.
I want the raw you, the you no one else grasps
because that's who I fell for, that's who I see.
So, let's not go back to small talk
Let go dive into the deep.

He sat there just a chair away, unaware
of the feelings he stirred inside of me.
In this car, I love to be.
Just a space where it's truly just him and me.
He stares and looks at me like
none had ever looked before.
I feel like this is the start of something new.
My heart pounding, my hands to their own.
I find myself revealing the crazy past that haunts
the daily life, I thought I tried to hide.
Hoping he won't see me for less – surprises me
Just one step closer. Holding tight, face to face.
A few mere moments in his embrace, I feel so safe.
If only he knew just how much he helped me see
I am a rose and not the thorn. A truth I fought at for so long.
I find it heavy on my heart, hoping he will understand
the moments of silence for no reason at all, none able to pull
me out of the wonder. They're the web my mind has woven.
There will be nights I question what he sees in me and lose
my balance, and nights I apologies for my own doing.
Unknowing to him I'll apologies repeatedly for me.
It's on the nights, when all feel lost, when I feel the world feels far away.
Where screams to the night sky holds the secrets of my soul.
All I will need is that one look. Just him across from me starting at all
I can be.

KELLY DE GUIA

I like your brown eyes behind the metal frames,
they're even better when you take it off.
I like your chocolate hair.
I like the way you smile and the way you laugh.
All I do is stare and think how joyful you are over there.
I like the soft kisses you give on my shoulder,
pulling me out of a trance a reminder that your near.
or when you rub my back and play with my long hair,
a feeling like none other stirs like when I watch Pooh Bear.
hope that 'doing nothing leads to the greatest something'
I like how excited you get when I tell you something small.
I like how surprised you were when you heard about my family history,
intrigued to learn more.
I like how distracted you get, when we follow a simple map.
Getting lost around the city streets still a favorite past time of mine.
I like how quickly you can change from handsomeness to sweet, from
boy to man.
I don't even think you know it.
Unaware of the looks you give that make me at time want to shy away.
I like the way you show off your supplements, at times I wonder,
do you really need them, I don't really care.
Take them, use them, just boy don't overdo them!
I like the way your face unknowingly glows when you talk
about programming and the work, you're doing.
I like the way you're on your own making it in the world,
against the crowd at such a young age.
I like the way you use your words, without knowing the impact they
are causing.
Do you know the impact of the words you sow?
I like the way you hold me; in your embrace I feel so safe.
I like how shocked you were when you first heard my interest,
to never forget the face, you made when mutual love for poetry was
shared.
I like how you take the time to come see me, for lunch, or just to check
if I'm okay.

I like the way I catch you staring, I want to know what are you thinking?
I like how unique your interest range from metal music to those scented
sticks.
I like the way you first said hey.
you don't know how much it made me look at things another way.
I like how you've always seemed proud at where I'm at in life
and still be excited for where I can grow.
I like the way you stayed when I told you about my jagged past.
I like how you call me yours, to hear that makes me weak.
I like how day by day whenever we're together I start to see
more of the man you are and the man that you can be.
They say there'll be one who'll pull you from the hole you're in,
who'll change the way you look at things.
I don't know if you're that one, but I know I'm better now that you're here.
I could go on for a long time to tell you how much I like you,
but I just want to learn you, ever bit of you.
I just want to hold and kiss you and tell you;
there's a lot of reasons why I like you.

..

KELLY DE GUIA

I met you on a cold wet rainy day,
the moment eyes had met
warmth like January nights took over.
My heart did not race, my hand did not find itself
twirling amongst my hair. Just one exhale and
there was rest, a calmness.
A moment of inner peace
that tonight was the start of something good
I noticed your eyes how blue they were, one day at lunch.
Just looking out, I caught myself staring,
thinking of a depth just like the sea we loved time spent.
A world I want to explore. A sense of adventure
waiting for me to open that door.
Knowing you brought about new identities
and questions to present realities.
days became month and months made up a year.
I've held on like all seasons in one since knowing you.
Winters warmth found in you brought about the bloom of spring
and the dawn of endless opportunities.
Summer night adventures rested as autumns leaves began to fall.
Just like the beauty of autumns letting go,
our leaves were shed, vulnerability exposed.
A mixture of the stress and shyness,
of questions kept and truths revealed.
You said it best 'this is different, it's something special'.
that's all I need, to know you saw the endless opportunities,
the excitement and adventure that was instore.
I do not know the look goodbye will have, or when
we one day will part. Maybe never, maybe just natural
like a growing sense of life.

In the midst of all the heartache
In the moments where thoughts run wild
with all the whys and what ifs?
all unanswered questions and silent moments of letting go

Love will find a way.

When life at times gets overwhelmed.
and months just crash overhead
When the act of crying feels like days.
When praying for the answer
just seems so dark and scary.

Love will find a way.

For love is not a person, love is not a moment
love is the memories we remember.
It's the words uttered expressing suppressed emotion.
Love's the randomness of laughter and the pride
with no guilt in saying sorry. It's the lack of anger in 'It's okay'.
It's dancing in the rain or snuggling by the sea.
It the breaking down on ones knees and the tight embrace
of not letting go.

It's in the unexpected twist and turns in life that love
will find a way. So, hold on to that memory
Keep tight to words that spoke,
it may be gone for now
but love will reappear just shortly.

Hold on, and cry till it aches, just remember
Love will find a way. Love will always find a way.

It's in the moments where he
just sits and stares, when that
small smile creeps upon his face
and the scent of lilies fill the air.
That I'm reminded of the beauty
in life simplicity. The cherished
life longings are the small moments
we don't notice in the business
of life.

My heart beats faster, my stomach flutters
Whenever you pull me close, whenever you are near.
It's the moment your lips touch mine,
or your hand runs down my spine,
I feel like I'm caught in the moment.
A mixture of excitement and fear.
The feeling of a giddy girl
seeing colors like none before.
Dancing with anxiety,
How quickly things can change,
Hoping it won't be taken away.
You told me once I'm Sadness & Beauty.
Do you see my sadness?
Is that the beauty you see when
you're staring back at me?
is that my sensitivity, or you
just seeing the private show.

There's a feeling that happens whenever you're about.
I'm like a girl, falling in love the first time around.
You hold me close; you pull me tighter
my heart beats faster and then it stops.
A peace and calmness a strange ease
in having you by my side.
Whether it be hand in hand or lips on mine.
There's a sweetness that envelopes me,
not the sweetness of sugared candy.
A sweetness in the fresh spring air or
the sweetness of sunshine in the rain.
That childlike, carefree feeling,
that's what you brought when you walked in
and said, 'hey long time no see'.
Security felt in your embrace; calmness when I'm wrapped up in you.
Waking up next to you or hearing goodnight come from your lips,
is like that first sip of coffee in the morning, even when its night.
You're the loudness and the silence, the beauty in the setting sun
and the thrill of adventure when it rises.
You're pleasantly different, I mean this in a compliment way.
Your eyes had depth, the brown showed the thought of caring and
adventure.
Excitement and fear, a clash of worlds but a learning curve,
to question current realities and insight to perspectives overlooked.
The hurdles of debate and the joy in respected arguments.
There's no story book character or movie star reference that captures
what I see in you and explain what you mean.
I hope my words don't fail me, I hope you already know,
you're someone who has changed me,
You're someone I am truly glad to know.

I wonder, I wait, I hope,
I seek a sign, a reminder.
Just something to show the way.
Will I? Won't I? Do it? Forget it?
Will you know? Will I fall?
Let it all crumble, be real, be true.
No longer hiding behind the mask I daily wear.
Exposed like the winter trees, standing still?

Who will he be? Who will I be?
When, today, tomorrow, when will it be?
So many questions, when will I get the answers.
like a whisper to the dark night sky.
'One day, someday', the response I often hear.
(So just not today)

Well are you ready, have you prepared?
Sigh and breathe, 'I do not know?'

'There's you're answer', someday, just not today.
Repeated several times. Still hope, no sign needed.
The voice inside a whisper is all you need.
One day I will know no need for alerts or clashing sounds.
That voice in the wind, the softness and the loudness
Will let me know that someday is today.

Bright lights and city streets there's chaos all around.
Crowds in all direction and yet I feel at ease.
There's a peace that's felt within.
Like magics in the air.
I'm home or right where I'm supposed to be.
Sirens wailing in the distance, music pounding from the corner club.
People walking, even running blurred faces in the whirlwind of spaces.
To the tourist, a night so spectacular, all looking to the harbor.
For there they see Sydney's beauty, the mask shown daily on display.
I go along the hidden routes, the laneways of unknown coffee smells and
the gardens of hidden bliss. I find myself strolling through familiar places,
taking time, when a meeting is an hour due.
I walk past all our favorite spots, the places we use to sit and laugh.
It now all foreign, like distant memories of another realm.
All of a sudden, I think of the chances, wondering when you last
strolled through. Questioning if you think about the tree, standing in
all its glory.
Caught laughing to myself, I continue coffee now in hand.
I know this path I am taking, wondering why I picked today.
I stop and see the bench we claimed once our own,
That day, I asked so stupidly 'is democracy on the exam list'
Thankful, you laughed and replied come sit and help me study.
Brought back to reality, the bench is just a short distance away.
The buzz in my pocket, the light of the screen, a name I haven't seen
in so long, surprised the number still saved on my phone.
'hello, look up ahead'
'it cannot be' 'it is, but how?'
how we both found our way back to the place where
it all began. I really do not know.
Maybe ending where it started is beautiful in itself.
Magic filled the air, as bright lights lit the quiet unknown city streets.
and maybe that's why I call it home.
For through the chaos of the cityscape.
I find beginnings where endings are also staged.

KELLY DE GUIA

Don't Speak, for once just give me silence.
Please no more excuses.
I already know. I saw the answer in the
drained color of your eyes. Your blue eyes no longer warm,
no longer like the skyline or the southern shore.
Something changed, never to be the same.

I felt the hurt in your embrace. No longer tight and secured.
Now knowing the space of safety and love
no longer mine, or a place to run and hide
when life got its saddened way.

I read the end in your text. The spaces spoke it all.
Words of time spent together now soaked
and filled with pain. I knew it was happening,
when minutes turned to hours of reply and read.

I heard my answer, when you said my name.
Knowing it will be the last time to leave your lips.
It all came together when I saw you sitting at the
bench, head between your hands. No longer
were there butterflies, just an odd stillness that remained.

I knew the combination of all, and felt the hurt in that hello
the first of goodbyes. Just two seconds
that sigh of truth revealed the reality of pain.
for once silence screamed where words stayed silent.
So please don't speak, no more lies, the truth revealed
Where words had failed, the end was evident in the
dark clouds above.

I hear the song come on the radio
Like every word sung is speaking of past memories.
I look out the small glassed window
to the blurred face of Sydney rushing pass.
My mind wondering to when we use to play
along the wood and shaded greenery.
I stroll through hidden streets, laneways and
cobbled paths, the ones people tend to miss.
and recall the laughter, embraces we shared.
I stand for a moment and stare out
to the bricked wall, the one underneath the bridge, to the corner
of the art paint bin. how crazy and foolish we once were.
Maybe that was love a vivid feel of excitement.
The sneaking off and being kids so stupidly in love, so close
and yet so far, the joke 'room for the holy ghost', still makes me laugh today.
The ferry honks, reality brought back;
a daily reminder, that's the past. For you're no longer here
or mine to hold. We don't keep in touch, I don't know where
you are today. These are just distant recollections of another life
we both had lived. No longer that couple, not even those people.
Just like the wall we hid behind. You're just broken promises
of yesterday. The song that plays, skipped for now.
Cause even though we've said goodbye, a small part still
Misses and hopes the best for the guy who broke me
and still could make me smile.

Heart stop fluttering, lips just don't speak.
Mind please don't overthink.
For once work for me and not against.
Another heartache I cannot take.
Don't blur the lines.
Don't cross the street.
You and him can never be.
A friendship so strong, let the feelings fade.
Don't destroy what's perfect, just walk away.
Support him, but don't need him.
Don't listen to the voice of romance,
You don't need the false hope, don't let
His expectations change, don't ruin the
Years you've worked on, don't let him hide away.
Heart stop fluttering, mind just go to sleep.
Don't destroy what's perfect.
Friends that's all that you both can be.

Sorry to disturb, it's the weekend, it's the break.
But I've been up for hours and crying to the song,
the one we laughed at, now on repeat.
Can't get myself to move won't even find myself
skipping the minutes that bring you back to me.
The lyrics overflow revealing all I kept aside.
You see I came home last night, rather three in the morning
after spending the hours with silence and nobody.
the night strolls when all asleep, I found myself awake.
I'm missing you and I'm blaming me, for loving you
when you no longer loved me. Not that I blame you
the fault was entirely on me. I put on the headphones,
sleep so far away, not the friend of mine today.
So, the music played, the lyrics screamed out.
Flashbacks vividly spinning around
A nostalgic trip came about, early hours ended
me in trouble. I'm calm on the outside, deep down
I want to cry. For I ignored you when you needed me,
Now I've lost you when I still want you.
It's been so long; I watched and did not stop you walking away.
Maybe I knew it then that a part of my heat will always be yours
even when I broke your heart many times ago.
I learnt the hard way; you only love it when you let them go.
It's been years since I've remembered you,
Months and days since I stopped crying over you.
So, I wonder why now you've reunited
within my heart and mind.
Cause I felt the lyrics, and everything just flowed.
Maybe it's the lonely hours, maybe it's the stress of today
the words spoke visions, the memories just poured.
There's nothing I can do, on the days where I miss you.
Cause what the hell did I do wrong, when loving you was
to be the main priority and I let it go.
All those years ago, when I thought its best If we remained as friends.
Now your gone, friendship never again, an option I deserve.

KELLY DE GUIA

Its 3am and I'm walking around the streets we use to know.
the lake still shimmers, and the wind still speaks your laughter in the breeze.
I'm sorry for it all. This will be the last
the song brings backs the memory of
you to my today. I loved you, then and even
now a small part of me will always stop when I hear
your name pass the lips of stories told. I loved you then
I learnt too late; you won't be here to help pull me through it all.
This message goes to the screams caught in the winds of today

They say it's better to have loved and lost
than to never have loved at all.
Yet here I am having loved and lost,
wondering if I could turn back time.
Go relive the moment when we walked away.
Wishing I could stop you, or stopped myself
from saying no. still can't find out why I let you go.
When you begged me to hold on, Cause I'm still in love with you.
I should have said the truth, when I had the chance,
to just see your face when we first say hi, the laughter
in familiarity.
A semester too long, became a semester too short.
I'm sitting here now, where we first made out
having loved and lost not feeling glad.
no sense of better in what's gone wrong.
For to have love and to lose it, A guilt none can change.
You left with the pain, left wrong of thought.
I left you with the memories, I'm now stuck on today.
To have loved and lost leaves me wanting someday,
to hope for a love, I won't have to ever lose again.

Every now and then I find you on my mind
remembering and questioning,
The I love you's, maybe and what if?
I need to stop and let it go
I need to leave the thought alone
(why can't it stop?)
Heart stop fluttering, whenever his name is said.
Mind just (let me) forget.
The face, the smile, the warm embrace,
No longer remember the depth behind them dark brown eyes.
They no longer make me smile, His arms no longer a running place
You were my then, but you're no longer my today, my now.
So please, oh heart, just say goodbye.
and leave the pain behind.

I'm sorry I got too straining,
I'm sorry you were always tired.
I'm sorry for the problems
I'm sorry I wasn't enough.
I'm sorry I did that.
I'm sorry I was part of the equation
That led you having to hide the daily stress.
All I ever wanted was to make you happy.
All I ever wanted was truth shared between you and I.
I know you said it's not me it's you, Boy it's cliché,
you know how I feel about the corny lines.
I can understand, but all I see is what I brought to you.
I never wanted to make you tired
I never wanted you to feel the pressure.
I never wanted to worry, question and say
at times the little white lies.
I never wanted to fall for you.
I never wanted to be impacted, to have you see me for who I truly am.
You broke down the walls, I found myself loving you.
I paid for it, the consequence of meeting you.
What once was joy now a mixture of anger and pain.
For now, it feels like months of happiness have shattered all around.
Darkness & Sadness is this phase.
I am sad that the time of truth has come along.
I am sad, we both saw it coming
I am sad that I can no longer have you.
I am sad that I lose the moments in your car, just sitting talking, laughing.
The silent moments of heated but subtle attraction
I am sad that I know there'll be the struggle of the new line now drawn.
We'll cross it on the drunken nights, just please no look of regret.
I'm sad that you won't be the boy for me, and I won't be the girl the
one to go all distance.
'It got to tiring, travelling from me to you'. that's what you said,
do you remember? we promised to hurt with the truth and never
comfort with a lie.

KELLY DE GUIA

I hated you for the truth.
I hate what I did to you, I hate that I don't hate you.
I hate that I am still so proud of you, still in your damn corner.
I hate that you're still the person I want to scream my news to
You make me feel like I'll accomplish anything, that facing giants
won't be so daunting. I hate that you still make me calm.
I hate that I still think of you, I still wish for your arms
when I'm sat having lunch with someone new.
I hate that I need you more than you ever need me.
So, I push it all aside because I want you still in my life.
A friend, a distant acquaintance, I'm just not ready to let go
One day we will say goodbye, I pray it happens naturally.

Maybe one day when I'm drunk or influenced by other stuff
I will tell you the truth. The hidden secrets and regretted lies.
Let out the parts of our story you still don't know
I will tell you how I felt that day and how I feel today.
I will tell you of the inner demons I had to daily face.
I will let you know the chance I took the night I said hello.
Maybe one day, I will tell you the truth, and hope you don't
look at me differently, no eyes of pity or hugs of sadness.
For that's the reason I held it so long.
I have told you how I'm grateful for you.
I have told you how you made me smile
I have told you that I'm always here, I'll still be on your side.
I have told you that you changed me, still unsure why?
Why you were a stranger, who soon became that guy,
my closest friend, that safe place. Why you became the sunshine
amongst the stormy skies.
For I know it got too much for you.
A struggle it had on me, to be the girl I thought you want
to please you at the sacrifice of me.
Stupidity or Gratitude? Is the answer really all so simple?
I do not know, and maybe never will.
I have said I am sorry, maybe too many times unknown to you.
but hey, 'I'm sorry' doesn't cover it.
Maybe one day, whether it be a month, year or five down
the line, I will tell you the truth. Sat around a fire, or in that
dimly lit alleyway, maybe in the middle of you laughing
I may tell you the truth, the hidden secrets of you and I.
Maybe one day I'll tell you how a boy like you came to save a girl like me.

KELLY DE GUIA

I had hope we lasted,
I had hoped for more time being us.
I had hoped for the world to finally be nicer.
I had hoped we both still see the worth we constantly see.
When looking at one another.
let's not remember the moments of sadness and pain,
Let this goodbye be different from the rest.
For once a chance to say hello.
if anything remember me in this way,
Remember me just snuggled next to you
listening to the rhythm of your heart as we listened
to the music play and watch the videos play on the screen.
Remember me just lying there, calm with your roaming hands
as the smell of jasmine fills up the room.
Remember me in the silent moments and
you pulled me close; no words needed
just a smile of assurance, the look to know I'm okay.
Remember all the laughter and surprise when we felt like
interest were aligned, so common and so rare.
Remember me through the words I've given you.
and the words you've sowed in me.
Remember me as someone who encouraged you
more than she encouraged herself.
If anything, remember me as your number one fan.
Remember the short getaways and the moments of pure amusement
more so at the jokes you made.
Remember the passion when you'd be the man and kiss me
along the wall, or in the street not caring what or who's around,
I'd pull you close and kiss you deeper. Remember that.
Remember the fun of hello, and the good in goodbye.
For I will remember the way you saw me, a light you turned within,

I'll remember the experiences I tried only through and with you.
I'm forever grateful for the moments you made me feel alive.
never knowing when you became the blessing and the curse
for forever I'll remember you. But a question remains,
Will you remember me even after goodbyes have been said.
Life

We can never truly forget anyone,
but we can release them.
Stop allowing past shared history
to impact our mood in the present day.
Why hold on and let the past dictate today.
Let go and continue to grow, to change.
No longer part of each other's life equation.
Continue falling & moving on.
Nothing wrong in meeting someone new.
Or spend the time to fall in love with you, the one who never left.
Don't hate them for letting go but thank them for what they showed.
You're stronger now because of them.
There'll be moment you remember the scent of his cologne,
as another passing in the air, laugh in remembrance of the
dance when that song plays on the radio.
Do not hate the time you were each other's main pride,
not every end is a failure.
Time will pass, life goes on, no thought of each other in so long
a moment will arise where you both will know.
the time will come, reunited, paths again entwined.
Maybe for a spare two second or a day of life doubt.
Whether we be distant strangers or old friends living now
states apart. New surroundings, change lifestyles being lived
a happiness now shared, a joy to know we cared.
Enough to let each other grow. No reason to be sad.
Our end was not a sign of failure, no fear and shame.
when that moment will arise, an unspoken pride will fill the air.
To know it's okay we let each other go, for love is happiness
with or without us there.

PART II

Life 'The Mountain & the Valley

For the highs and lows, and moments between, mountains and valleys, and rivers and streams, for where you are now and where you will go [...] Its here in this journey you will learn to be strong, you will get where you are going, landing where you belong.
- MHN

THERE IS A Greek word called 'Metanoia' meaning the journey of changing ones mindset, heart, self or way of life. A spiritual conversion. The context of the word comes about to originally discuss the repentance of an individual life, but when I came across this word for the first time all I read was a journey of change, 'changing of ones mindset', and thought that is the basis of what life is, right? That at the end of our years we reflect and realized we have gone through many seasons of change and many conversations with ourselves on life, love and faith. I don't know what the best summary of life could be but this one does a good job.

Growing up my dad had instilled many life lessons into my childhood, but the biggest one my siblings and I all greatly remember and will continue to remember when it comes to having our own families is the lesson of choices, 'choices we make in life'. The concept that however our life may turn out, it will be based on the choices in our lives; whether they be good choices or bad choices, they were always our choices that we made, our metanoia of life.

However long or complex the journey, despite if it may feel like we spend more moments in the valley rather than on the mountain tops, life will be seasons and none will ever be the same. The hope that we will continue to walk the journey in changing mindsets and in growing. Our journey, our vision of our desired outcome, will always change depending on the season and on the mindset, we find our self in, what we deemed as happiness can differ from childhood innocence to the high buzz found in our twenties. What we chased after may become something different. Life has to be more than the cliché lines we all read and recite; it has to be unique it has to be more. Like the lesson my dad taught me life is made up of our choices, we may not see the impact of the choice straight away, but we will. Life will make sure that every action will have its reaction. I am not saying life is so black and white, it's not. Life is something different to every person. What I see my life now as and what it will look like six months, a year even 10 years is uncertain, I guess that's the thrill right? The fact that its never so clear. That life won't be as simple as a rollercoaster ride or a box of chocolate. What I do know is that there is a difference in existing and in living.

If you haven't guessed by now, the words that have been spoken over my life or even just proclaimed in and around have touched me, have stirred something and have made me think about life about my own relations about my own perspectives. That's the power of the words and the impact a simple line of arranged words can have on any individual. So, another story. One day I was thinking, what can I say about the mountain and valleys of life and I remembered a moment not long ago. I was having lunch with a few friends, it was a reunion of sorts, we had all graduated university, we were all now working full time, thrown into the whirlwind of adult hood; yet as we sat for hours and just caught up we realized we all had something to whine about. Adulthood and living life was not what we pictured when we were studying. During that lunch, a friend was like serious question, are we living or just existing? The question soon turned out to be a joke, like we all imagined it would be, but I left that lunch thinking deeply on that, *'are we living or just existing'*?

The quote by MHN outlines how life is that mixture of everything. The underlying essence of this book. The mixture of the sadness and beauty in any moment of life. if I was asked that question today, in my current life I would say I have done both, at the same time and one over the other. I have had moments where I experience or feel like I am truly living, that every day is another adventure. Where I have been able to grow, able to change able to look fear in the face and laugh at how strong I am, I have been able to laugh till I cry and just experience the moment in all its glory. Where life truly has been sunshine and rainbows. Here I find myself saying yes to life, just experiencing the gratitude of everything around me. But there have also been moments when I find myself in the valley when I know now that I wasn't living but I was just existing, doing things for the sake of completing and the sake of living. I was in my depths and just not bothered, which started to show externally and internally, passion for writing was turning into frustration, interest disappeared, and time spent alone was increased. Growing up as a kid, sleep was something that I hated, always wanted to stay up late, to play till the sun went down, and then there were moments when sleep was my best friend. Unable to look at the duties and the passion of today and take hold of it, I would rather just shut my eyes, and let the world pass me by.

Do I hate myself for the moments of just existing since I cannot take back time, well yes but also no. because its also in the valleys, in the seasons of nothing and silence that I was able to learn about myself, learn about support and realize who was speaking truth when they said they'd be there and who was just saying what I wanted to hear, and maybe that's growing up and life doing its thing. Maybe not everyone I meet will be there for life, and I am only learning now that sometimes that's a good thing. I have been on this journey on earth for a quarter of a century, have I got it figured out, no, does anyone really have life figured out. I mean there are the small aspects that I know and hope that I am being real, to myself and to the people who have always been there for me.

The following poems show the change of perspective and change of thought that I have gone through. You know what I have learnt in life? I have learnt that we need someone to journey with us, to critique us, to yell and shout, out of love out of hatred, but to also laugh with, this might be a group of people it may be just one individual, but I have learnt life is not meant to be journeyed alone. How dull life is to be walking alone. It's a cliché right, I am trying my hardest not to sound like another motivation book, but in all seriousness maybe those self help books make sense, I have read some over the years from faith based to science based and a common aspect they all discuss is mindset, when you are happy, everything falls into place, or that's what they say. I guess in some way there is a truth in that. Happiness is if not the greatest motivation, a great source of hope but there is still a question of, what does being happy look like? I have had those times when happiness was easy to identify. Like in a crowd of strange faces, I would be able to pick out happiness with the connection of inner joy and I have also gone through moments where happiness was faked, or where it was a lie. Not that I don't appreciate those moments where I may have been glad to be alive, or content, but it were these moments where truth and hurt were deeply felt. There is a difference between being content and being happy, like the question asked by my friend are we living or just existing. I have found the hurt of truth and the frustration in reality, like a punch in the face. A review of my life journey truthfully there have been moments where I was content and that was my border, because I was scared of losing, scared of being alone. There have been memories where I can look back on pictures and videos and know deep down, I was happy in that moment, that everything that went on was all out of genuine feelings. It was the mountain and the valley together and by itself.

LIFE

THE MOUNTAIN & THE VALLEYS

As she sits there in the shade waiting
the minutes tick away. She looks around
at silence, nothing but stillness surrounds
(she does not panic).
Just breathe (she breathes)
Sound intensifies, now her company for the day.
She looks and hears the howling wind,
roaring through the dense green trees.
She remembers innocence in the chirps of the
many birds, singing natures daily song.
She notices the beating, the rhythm of her heart.
A sudden realization, as she sits there in the wait.
Calmness is her silence. Peace now surrounding her.
for the first time in a long time, now within her mind.

KELLY DE GUIA

Change, something that happens.
Something we cannot avoid, stop, or delay.
Change will hurt us; it will scare us.
Embrace it or run away, it won't go far away.
Change will shape us and bring about new growth.
Change a good thing or a bad thing?
Not so simple maybe a mixture of them both.
Change is life, we cannot move ahead
without the journey in the change.
Take hold and just watch it cultivate,
Change may amaze you; Change may surprise you.
Cannot control the change that happens,
Change won't control the way we feel.
Change is inevitable. Change is growing up in life.

Balloons, the plastic spheres of lovely colors.
The universal image for times of joy
A symbol of celebrations and thanksgiving.
Childhood parties to the school street fairs.
Smiles you tend to see, in the joy and spark
found in young children's eyes.
How bright they shine when given just one.
Those colored spheres of random happiness.
It's in the cackle of laughter when they float along
the party floor then randomly Go POP!
surprise and funny faces, the few leaps of shock around.
Balloons are not specific to one age,
Balloons can tell more than just a decorative tool.
Do you notice the depth it holds,
How at times we fail to see the other side
of somber sadness and vulnerability
balloons at times strongly represent and hold.
There's a farewell felt in the colored spheres.
A sadness when we let go and watch them disappear
above into the sunlit sky. The letting go of pass mistakes;
remembrance of all held dear, a loved one or a burden kept too long.
Just let it go and watch the balloon fade away.
The quiet stillness of observation, now a symbol
of release and letting go from childhood foolishness
to the sorry of today, visual of that goodbye.
No tears are shed just the balloons that drift
carrying the secrets and regrets of yesterday and today.
I guess balloons are more than just the ordinary party prop.

KELLY DE GUIA

A pen is filled with ink, look beyond the plastic
tube and all the different types, felt tip, ball pen,
that's not of importance. Think beyond material
and see the magic that overflows.
Such power all from the tip of another pen.
Twirled between my fingers or pointed at lined paper.
Stories of sadness and adventure soon take over.
Defining moments, signed sealed and delivered,
the final memories made with the thing
chucked, tossed or left around the floor, like an object
of no importance, stuffed between the padded couch.
Do you see the importance in the small but mighty thing?
We at times so easily replace.
For laws are made and stories that can be overtold.
How pens have been used to start lives and end hostile wars.
To mold new chapters and tear down negativity.
from twirling to tapping (my made-up drumsticks).
Marks of my body, marks on my paper.
Pen so small and yet so powerful but still so not well kept
Blue, black, green or red all different meanings, all different powers/
The red of correction and mistakes, a tool of learning.
blue to simply journal memories of emotion, the joy in writing.
capturing what could not be said. The ability
to read what's felt the moment spent a day, month or year ago.
The formality and boldness in the color black. Significance and
statue like seriousness and hype. Just look beyond the plastic
tube, look beyond the tool, think deeper and you'll
notice the magic that it keeps, the power overflowing through the
simple gadget tossed and found all over the floor.
For a pen is truly mightier than the sword

We were driving one day along the road, greenery all around
a road that that became the daily view,
same old dirt roads and thick greenery to both our sides.
until I saw the diamond in the rough, the outlier. I saw a cloud.
It was no ordinary cloud, not like the others in the day sky,
This one knew its difference, it seemed to spread on for
what seemed like miles. It was one I knew I'd remember.
One I knew I'll never see again.
So many layers, many different parts.
Overflowing waterfall, stationed just above.
Sitting, basking in all its glory.
A sense of curiosity and gratefulness
suddenly filled the air, expectation of the day.
A decision made, to pull over.
witness nature doing its splendid thing.
The white long cloud, so low like we could reach out and grab it
In the south sky, sitting in its grandeur.
Knowing the show, it had to perform.
It was a day I can vividly replay.
A season of business through camper vans and rushing cars,
untouched by the stillness we found ourselves.
Standing for a few more minutes, shock or wonder.
Maybe both?
Marveling at what was ahead of us, something now came over.
indescribable feeling, no words, nothing but this moment.
Just standing there, with wet hair, the smell of sea
Still on me. That minute in a random lot, pulled in by the wonder
of the unusual cloud. Slowly, but visibly it started dissolving.
The cloud was saying its final goodbye.
It was a short yet beautiful affair, a marvel at what a fete it
was to witness, oh a cloud for an unusual day.

Hold on they say, hold on, hold on, hold on,
against the push and pull life brings our way
I look out to the harbor shore and to the leaves
on the rustling trees, a beauty in the chaos,
A sense of pride in the falling leaves of May.
Autumn in its glory, like flame of no danger,
Sweeping through the densest trees,
Shining all its ambered colored, like soldiers
Marching away, there's a hero's fate in the
Falling leaves that crunch beneath our booted feet.
As I sit in its glory, to pick one up and hear that
Smallest voice, well done in letting go.
Like the beauty that autumn brings our way.
a beauty in the act of letting go.
Holding on may not always show such strength
and bravery, but a sense of sacrifice and pain.
What if we like autumn leaves of May
just take our weakness and let go.
LET GO, LET GO, LET GO.
That leap of faith, the free fall of ending
Any sense of pain.
For if there is a lost, I guess there must be a found
that comes along and exists like the sides
of the coin we toss in the air. *I guess I'm just not there.*
there's courage to be on the way, when the lapping
waters reflect a peace within my inner core.
Just like the cup filled with tea, I hope my world
Bring endless possibilities, so let go just like
The autumn leaves of May.

My watch broke down today.
I saw something for the first time,
It took a while, but I saw the moment
the ticking stop. When life gave out and brokenness
was all that the watch now left.
I found myself thinking how hard it is
When it comes to humans like you and I.
How brokenness can go unknown,
undetected days and months in a row.
When did broken begin,
When did life internal clicking stop?
I viewed my watch life just halt, the ticking paused,
No longer time told. The watch 11:05
Forever stuck at five past eleven. Bju, lmoikjhytbjoi
Does brokenness look like a watch, stopped clicking.
Will it be known? Will those around see the halt, repair it on the go
or only notice when its already gone. Brokenness so evident.
I guess I learnt a lesson from my broken watch today.
How easy it's to see and fix a broken clock,
then a broken you and me.

My favorite life moments are not pictures of glitz and glam,
of moment where we find ourselves dressed from head to toe.
Those second where I forget just what I'm doing,
just happy to be out and about dressed for the world to see.
No, my favorite moments are opposite of those.
They are the moments life comes undone,
the ones not caught on camera kept private,
to in the moment, a secret of sorts kept for only us to know.
They are the moments when one word brings back all
The feels, all emotion whether it be sad or glad.
How quickly present reality impacted by the spoken past.
It's the raw moments in life, like a badly worded joke,
in the midst of all, laughter could not be contained.
Crinkled corners around our eyes, fanning hands
and sneaky snorts, the tears of laugher and gasps of air.
Like we wish the world was in on this, to know the reason
Why we at times look like crazy fools, but the covering
of mouth with our hands, show its best a secret kept.
It's the moments of sadness where tears just overflow.
The moment when grief is all we consume, visibly
The deflation is all that shows, from shakes and body aches.
To exhaustion of the tissues thrown, it shows the depth
of the ones we loved and the people we at times had to walk away.
I remember the darkest days, when misery was my only present
company, how isolated and alone I felt. And at times still feel, but
like winter ends and spring begins I remember the rising sun and
the hope that springs, like seeping slowly in, the laughter in reality
'the best is yet to come'.
Its those moments found at random hours of the night,
walking along the quiet lanes, or 2 am calls.

It's the 5am wake ups to start weekend adventures. Where whispers of fear and shouts of joy are mixed and told, sometimes found to dance around along the edge of the very cliff, we released and said goodbye. To let go and here it echo into the darkened sky. Its all these moments, its all the raw and realness that I remember, moments where we laughed and cried moments of no words but realness in the observation. Its in the unimaginable I find myself at times. These are the moments I will remember, the toughness and the ease. The laughter and the tears. I remember all.

What makes up a human body?
Limbs, joints, muscle, blood and veins
all joined together, pumping out night and day.
Look a little deeper enzyme and atoms,
flow around, all unseen to the naked eye.
There's a muscle as big as your own fist,
that sits there right down the middle
beating ever second, ever minute, our
daily source of life. Nothing like the drawings
of the two year old, or adults when they celebrate
the day of love, look a bit closer and you will see
the veins, the pipes the ugliness that's confronting.
Words like ventricles and septum, vital for surviving.
all flow through the middle muscle the one we call the heart.
Emotions is that what makes us human. The brain the goo
of knowledge so much power.
Damage you're a couch potato.
Limbless and unresponsive, the life you lived now down
the drain. How great I guess it is to be hardheaded.
Then there's chromosomes, a word that falls right off the tongue.
All we grow to be from molecule things, all the X and the Y, questions
of the dating realm. Makes us who we are.
Perception changes on our upbringing.
Values, faith or beliefs, no longer seen to be direct, difference
is the choice still our or science to make. ATCG 26 makes our
identity, can't choose our genes, like we do daily, not like the skinny
or the straight, ATCG the ones that make our history.
All codes in the biology, one within the other.
So, what makes up the human body?
Science or emotion, love or heart. Maybe both, maybe just one.

Maybe I'm an old soul,
still wanting to believe in the chivalry of love.
Maybe I'm an old soul,
that still tears up at the simplicity of life.
How the simple pen and paper overwhelms my soul.
To see blankness of pages soon be filled with emotion of the seasons lived.
Lined in poetic sentences. Words waiting to come out.
Maybe I'm an old soul
Who won't quit when things get hard. to fight for what I stand for.
but wise to know there'll be moments better to stay quiet
knowing spoken words in that moment may turn to regret.
Maybe I'm an old soul who loves the turning of a page,
over the scroll of a lit-up screen.
Evidence in the wrinkled pages and faded coffee rimmed stains.
The importance of storytelling in the character of evidence remained.
Maybe I'm an old soul,
who still finds creativity among land of greenery.
Maybe I'm an old soul, who feels the peace in cold crisp winter walks.
Maybe I'm an old soul still foolish to believe in the Christmas spirit or the
loved up tale of time standing still.
Maybe I'm an old soul, who believe the power of I love you and I need you.
Maybe I'm an old soul, who feels the emotion when the lyrics
overcome the thoughts and sing what I cannot say.
Maybe I'm an old soul, who still believes the best is yet to come.
Maybe despite all that is changing, being an old soul, is just who
I really am. I feature I willingly accept. No longer maybe.
Yes, I truly am an old soul.

I want to think of dangerous and noble things again.
Be carefree, light, to dance and twirl in empty streets
or the safety of my bedroom walls. No care of judgement.
but freedom to just be that quirky, dorky me.
I want to soar amongst the fluffy clouds and stand in beauty
like wildflowers blooming, growing in their own accord.
Just show radiance in the unexpected places.
I want to be spontaneous, throw away night plans,
and embrace the randomness of the minute.
Make the most of the moment I am in.
To walk the words I think I live, from carpe diem to smile despite
the hardship of it all. To not speak the empty hollow promises that
hurt me once before.
To not be held by the fears of life, a hope for ease to saying yes
to all the things I double question.
To no longer doubt the good that comes my way.
I hunger for the days to return when we danced in the rain
or sang in the shade. The moments where laughter turned to tears,
not out of sorrow or that sense of loss, but of joy and inside jokes.
I need the moments of memories, where I can write or take a snapshot,
and still feel joy, laughter or pain when I come across the picture
once more in today or tomorrow.
I want for the innocence of a childlike perspective,
To still be active despite my adult life.
To hope my youth does not fade with the rise of age.
I hope for live and not just exist.

I know there'll be a day we will have to say
all the things we tried to keep at bay.
I know there'll be a moment when we will
meet death straight in the face. I hope that
when the moment will pass and come
for me to say my final goodbye, I can
confidently reply 'I'm okay let's go, I lived
and felt all I could be and do. I'm ready to go home'.
instead of realizing just how late, deflated and
annoyed, to hopefully not have to sit and plead,
'Oh, please just one more life, I promise I'll be quick,
there's things I forgot to do and words I never said.
How will they know I loved them; I now cannot let them go'.
I hope that when I meet deaths face, I'll take that sigh
and smile, the final breath and know it's done, I have
finished the final race. That those who know will feel
the celebration and continue the life I daily hope to lead.
That my words will resonate in time, that there'll be the days of
silent laughter in moments that we shared.
For I know the day will come, when goodbye is final.
so, I hope that when death comes my way,
hello, won't be so scary.

All I want is someone to tell me it's okay not to be okay.
That sometimes sadness is needed.
that days spent resting are not shameful.
It's okay to watch the movies that make you cry,
I want someone to tell me it's okay to weep and yell
to let it all out to scream until it aches,
till you're tired from release of all that you held near.
I want someone to tell me it's okay to want to be alone,
to ignore the world around just once a while.
To ignore the messages and repeated calls, to not
need to lie when asked, is everything okay? Excuses getting slim
I want someone to tell me it's okay to have that moment
where the only thing left to do is shout out all inside frustration.
To just let all caged anger out, let it echo to the night dark sky,
Like howling wolfs and honking horns. That the loudness is
out and not the loudness in our heads.
I just want someone to tell me it's okay not to be okay.
That weakness is allowed from time to time.
Just show my hidden fears, remind me I'm not alone.
I just want someone to tell me it's okay to be lost
to be unsure, of what the future does in fact hold.
It's okay to not have life or the next five months
figure out, that the uncertainty was the thrill
of their best life adventures. That it's the failure
that some best memories are held,
that a silver lining is not a rare sight to hold.
I want someone to tell me it's okay not to be okay.
Cause one day these days will be the ones I'll
be grateful for, the days I survived the worst.

Because no one else has said this,
I might as well say it to myself.
For when the day will come,
I know I'll be okay.
I'm sorry, sorry you desperately try to fix others
making sure they're in one piece, despite the shaking
of your own hands, the stitching you as well need.
I'm sorry healing became so rushed, where the ones you cared,
were bandaged hands now wounded. Fixed despite
yourself just bleeding, no band aid or hidden tools.
I'm sorry for the forceful smiles and the awkwardness
of faked laughter. So, the moment won't be ruined,
for you know they don't need another problem,
enough on their own plates.
I'm sorry repeatedly for all the time and love you gave,
to people who didn't really care. Where love to them
was just a game, they would win, and you would lose.
To love too much with nothing in return.
I'm sorry you thought that was the love you deserved.
I'm sorry to the silent nights left alone, you found a
way to cry yourself to sleep. Where no one bothered
or tried to understand.
Why each day, your bed is where you spent
long hours to pass away.
I'm sorry that you're going through this,
all alone, I'm sorry I could not show you
how much I really liked you. How your intelligence is
not to hide but to be displayed day by day.
I'm sorry that you felt the bottom when you should
have felt the top. I'm sorry for the constant silence
even if they still don't; notice the pain in their halfhearted
promise of I'll always be there.
I hope you can see it, just how much I like you.
How much you deserve the love you dream and read about;
not just fantasy but your day reality. I'm sorry I did this to you,
I'm sorry I can't believe I did this to my own. Kelly I'm sorry.

When everything has passed there'll come a moment.
When you look back and know you have survived.
No certificate or big parade,
just a simple breath to say it all.
You'll see the dignity in knowing you made it,
passed and crossed the line.
Made it to the moment you never thought you'd be.
That the day has come and you're standing tall.
It may be when no image plays your head.
It may be when tears finally turn to laughter.
It may be the exhale of one final release.
Take pride in knowing, you made it through,
That even diamonds go through pressure, and
Beauty they're forever known.
How much stronger the hurt and pain now makes you.
The doubts you listened to for so long will be silence.
That even when a day not good, you'll know
There's still good in the day that come and gone.
Change perspective, sun still shines amongst the rain.
That pain, though hurtful and unnerving,
made you fight till you succeeded.
Maybe today, is not that moment, maybe not now, not even tomorrow
But the day will come when you look back on all
the things that broke you, all the pain you ever felt and
they will be the things you're forever grateful.

I often sit and wonder, when people read
the words we right, if they can feel all
emotion that was felt. From the sadness
to the joy, does it rush through them, just like
It overflowed the minute pen did touch paper.
Can they picture the surrounding, like the dense
green trees and curled tracks hidden behind the
story house. Do they picture themselves in that
adventure of the past memory. How lines of silent
walks along the river shore are moment of inner peace.
or the stains and damp corner pages show the release
of pain with every word that's written down
do they see the space between the words, and wonder
of the hidden screams of anger and frustration, the many
moments of wanting help before it's too late.
Do they see such power behind the simplicity in how words
like I love you at times easily turn to I hate you...
How I am sorry lost all meaning and sorry replaced
with F**K YOU! I wonder if they fell the pain in every goodbye
that they have read, or the joy in every hi.
For when I read the words of others, I often find reflection
in the stories felt, so I often sit and wonder what they feel
when reading on our daily lives, do they feel the emotions
I have felt.

KELLY DE GUIA

A question was asked one lunch time what is a moment you like to repeat?

We went around the table and it was the typical answers you'd expect,
a defining moment in everyone's life whether it be their wedding day,
their favorite holiday, the moment they fell in love. All defining days.
Until it came to me, A moment I would repeat would be

'It would be that moment before the sun rises when it's not yet fully out,
still like a little kid playing peekaboo,
but it makes sure the early ones know it's time for a new day.
The moment you can see the color hit the greenery of the trees
as if it's dancing with the leaves.
As it mingles with the shadows of the night before
that still linger on for just a few more minutes.
It's that moment where it changes the color of the skies
the mixture of blue and yellow, no longer that midnight darkness of
mystery,
the shadows go back to sleep as light begins to dance.
It is for these few moments, that I love to repeat
It's like I see the world for what it truly is;
a mixture of the dark times and the good times.
but there's this undeniable light making sure all will know
it's one for light to shine, a diva of sort cause once it's there nothing
can hide,
it reaches the densest of places and still mingles there amongst them.
It truly touches all. It's like all of nature is shown in a different beauty,
from going through the journey of darkness to lightness.
It's in this moment before the sun truly says good morning
that I can see all the dreams of yesterday whisper to the hopes of today
it's the moments where you can truly see the two worlds collide.

I'm just a girl wanting to belong.
To feel noticed, thought of and made aware.
A chance to finally be the girl, he loves to not
ruin every good with fear of past mistakes.
I want these fears to go away, never to return.
I want the victory to outshine the failure that I see.
I want the thought everyone leaves to not
be my current reality. Grateful for the ones who still
stay, despite the number, its more than I enough.
To stop the over thinking, analyzing;
worst case scenario not a daily thought.
I want when conversations come my way
to not scare away and feel shamed about my brain.
Intelligence must be embraced.
I just want the strength to say enough. For courage to say
I too need help. I want to look up at the sky and think
of childhood memories, feel peace once more against
the crashing waves. I want to live to my potential,
the goals all marked as complete.
I'm just a girl still trying to find my way.
Hoping one day I'll have the voice to say
'it's okay, now let all negativity go'.

KELLY DE GUIA

Expendable! No real significance.
Able to be easily destroyed.
Maybe even just abandoned
Expendable.
How easy do we do this
to the people that we know,
the ones we say I love you,
and its ok, I'm there.
It's the word I see when I stare
back at me, the one I often
run to when asked what defines me.
Expendable.
For how easy I am left alone
Forgotten a nonpriority.
Just a friend, a stranger I suppose.
busy but I see your status.
No ask or thought am I okay?
Abandoned so many times before.
I'm not perfect, I know I've done the same
I'm sorry, for the feeling of expendable like me.
Why act so surprise when I say the fear of failing
or loving you stop me on the daily.
There's an accepted hurt it's what's deserved,
For me and from me, I'm sorry once again.
Expendable.
Scared history shall repeat, if only
there was proof to show incorrectness
in my lame ass speech. Maybe this
is on myself, but no connection still is made,
No red bubbles of messages read or sent,
Do you think I hope she is ok? I wonder.
Expendable.
Unlike Sylvester, forgotten I shall be.
Cause like the word says, no real significant,
able to be destroyed. Expendable is all I see.

All I hope for is remembrance
What a blessing and a curse,
the gift remembrance really is
for remembrance brings both
pain and joy, times of sorrow and
moment of uncontrolled laughter.
I hope to not forget the moments
where I wept, a mixture of both
heartbreaking ache or laughter
that turned into tears. For they will
show the hardest scars and the moment
when the walls were down, exposing
me for who I truly can be.
I long for remembrance, to keep
track of all the stories lived, the moments
where night adventures showed a life
that's rarely lived, the dancing in the tunnel
to the music that echoed through, to the
random dinners with strangers turned international
friends. I hope for remembrance to all the
loves I have met, the ones who taught me
how to love and the annoyance to remembrance
of the ones I want to forget.
I hope for remembrance to my own name,
or more so the deed I do, in my daily life.
Hoping that when my name is said, goodness
may remain, that only times of laughter and not
times of pain, vividly play, whenever my name
gets thrown into the rain. For one day will fade
with the secrets of the evening breeze.
I hope for remembrance to people I have met,
remembrance in what they installed, the lessons
that they had told. All I hope for is remembrance for
humanities simplicity.

KELLY DE GUIA

How simple life would be in a black and white world
like the many hung photographs lined along my
bedroom wall. Each one showing such vulnerability
like a daily depth we don't usually see, in a fascinated colored world.
Would fear and disappointment still hurt the same,
not seeing color drain from our loved ones faces.
or hurt when all we see is dullness in their eyes,
when truth and sadness are revealed.
Would joy escape the moment of awe and beauty in
natures daily dance when diamond crystals shimmer
in sunlight amongst the cloud and rainy days.
Would New Years Eve still fill us with excitement
when no color slows through the dark velvet sky?
Will spring still bring about the sense of hope
without the shades of blooming flowers?
Would life truly be so simple if we lived
amongst a black and white world?

On a crisp autumn day, leaves are falling all around
I remember letting go can be unseen beauty found
Where hurt more felt in struggling to not touch the ground.
Evidence in the falling leaves beauty in the end.
It's the chilly winter nights, so still and cold
that teaches life's simplicity. Silent moments of
observation bring about a season of much needed rest.
Slowed down and truly have that desired break.
I tend to see winter nights as moments of inner clarity.
The time of spring and new beginnings, a chance to start
afresh, as woken creation sing again all of nature's hymns.
The yearly reminder life starts again, the sun still shines,
The death of winters chill will come to an end.
A step of faith or spring of new, more to all life hurt and pain.
I feel lessons to the walk of life, greatly on a summers day.
The streets of laughter and bike rings, bring back youthful days
life knows it's still okay, despite the lows, the highs will hold
place. Life really a mixture of seasons, never ending, always
repeating, never coming just the same. Winter, spring summer
or fall, I guess you need one to know all.

KELLY DE GUIA

When things don't go the way we plan,
I must believe there's purpose to the failure.
To hope its okay to have a moment of unknown,
that life whys at time need no answers.
To learn and realize that sometimes plan we make
will be at times the ones that fail.
Looking back, we'll understand how good things
can come from failed strategies.
Unknown now, you'll come to understand, that time
is not ours to control, never truly on our side.
It will always hurt when doubt enters the place you
worked to have no hold, but pressure and strain
can go beyond the naked eye. Blind by love or
the pressure to succeed, truth at times harder
than the comfort of a lie. I have to believe
that I don't always get what I want, but I will
at times get what I just need, maybe I don't know
It until its already here. To hope that in failure and
irritated patience lessons of life are learnt and felt.
That in the silence we hear our answers.
I have to believe that when life does not go the way
we planned, that the end is just another hidden start.
At times it's in failure that truth be revealed.
Maybe not now not even tomorrow. It may take time,
it may be like a badly worded rhyme, but with age
you come to understand moments of failure,
may be disguised moments of success.
That nothing's wrong in taking time to heal, to cry until our body aches,
to laugh until we snort and cry. To grow and change from
who we were five years before, Hope and see joy in the misdoing.
I have to hope that each hurdle is a lesson we continue to learn.
That the moments in our valleys, help understand the mountain tops.
That praise is only possible through the struggle we fought and faced.
It may be in silent observations that we understand
how perfectly imperfect it is okay to not be okay. Every
hour of every day. I need to hope the best is still to come.

The rustling wind and loudness of the thunder,
The random cackling of lighting outside the glassed window.
Where nerves and fright are normal sights, peace comes over.
She breathes and silently looks out
listens to the rumble in the night and stormy sky,
the sky flashes like photography,
expose the shadows dancing in the trees.
Just silence in staring out she wonders
about recent discoveries.
The life decisions recently she has made.
and just like that the rain pours down
the sound of patter on the roof
she loves this moment when thoughts and memories come alive,
like in her room vividly to dance around and make her ponder.
In the silence, the sound of thunder echoes in her room.
Declaring all support to the decision
that she has kept on thought.
Unsure about tomorrow,
still stuck remembering yesterday.
Just like the storm raging on the
other side of the wall, the peace
fades and reality shows its face.
Just like the loudness of the storm
Her screams do fade, if she does not burst too late.

KELLY DE GUIA

Why do I feel like crying, why do I continue sighing.
I have everything I need, all the wants that I have craved.
Why continue to act this way?
I'm sorry in advance, to the people who have loved me.
I wake up each morning a quarter past three,
the random hour, a mind of doubts, questions and memories.
Unsure of my current state, I know I wish to be in his embrace.
This not your burden to uphold, not your problem anymore.
So, I'll act the way you want me to, I'll smile and wave,
Happy as I can be, hoping it'll be my truth.
To stop hiding, behind the mask I wear.
just be myself, I wish that be my reality.
Its selfish, I know. Wrong? for sure.
Make me ungrateful, makes me forgetful?
For all the current good that comes my way.
You are for me, not against me.
So why no difference when I say it on repeat.
When I'm with you genuine smiles I have, but one is not enough
one still won't change the hurt and pain I feel inside.
I'm lying and its unfair, but no one's there.
Who's to listen none really care.
Cause I'm happy, I'm blessed (supposedly)
But why still now do I feel like nothing comes my way.

*****written as two parts, within the space of 2 years from 2011 to 2013*

PART I

All it takes is just one leap.
All it takes is just one moment,
To take that second and just breathe
Inhale... exhale (on repeat)
To fall, to halt, to start that project
you kept on pause.
something you always wanted to just try, and step into the unknown
No fear of failure do something you never thought to do.
Take the step and not look back,
To live the life with no regrets
All it takes is just one giant step....

PART II

I took that step; I don't look back.
I hear the knock of past at times so loud and so soft.
I took the leap to something new. All has changed
never the same will life be again.
I'm happy and excited, fear remains just not as much.
Life still has the why? But unanswered I'm okay
I inhaled and grabbed the moment by hand,
chased it till I grasped it.
Exhaled to the beauty of another defining minute.
Fear or intrigue? (maybe both) Excitement and the nerves
Just a moment, that's all it took, just 3 seconds
life forever changed. The course of journey
now gone another way. All it takes is just one leap
and step into the unknown.

.

KELLY DE GUIA

We are just a speck of dust
in a universe so vast.
Still so much undiscovered,
Still so much to discover.
So, if we shout out all the trials,
all problems that we lock inside
a hidden vile, will we be heard over
curiosity and intrigue, will we be remembered.
Questions of the whys and how?
Maybe one is not the other
is there a point to any of this?
Maybe life just like a star
just waiting living daily to explode.
TICK TICK BOOM
Is our end as beautiful as the exploding star?
In a world so vast we are nothing but a speck of dust.

They say we are influenced by our surroundings
Made up of the stories felt and lived, from
Childhood moments to the adult life we wake up to daily
There are many things that have molded and prepared me.
I am the mixture of past and present, with hope for tomorrow.
Who am I? I am the combination of all experiences,
The moments of joy and memories of tear soaked tees.
I am a constellation of all conversation
with people I have met from young childish days,
to grown up parties in different states. I am the hurt
of hollow words and broken promises but also the laughter
from inside jokes and words of affirmation.
I am made of the happiness shared with friends and all arguments
with mom and dad. The moments I needed them and moments
I was annoyed at how right they were,
just not known in that moment of youthful pride.
I am the brokenness and stitching of past loves and current hurts.
Mixed with the kindness of strangers, reminded of humanity.
I am the bitterness of regretted words I cannot get back,
I am the infatuation of loved confessions and the pride in my intellect.
I am a mixture of the mountains and the valleys.
I am all things felt and all things I wish at times that I could forget.
The simplest smile to another in-depth conversation
That is who I am, that combined makes me, who I am.

PART III

Faith

"I believe in Christianity as I believe that the sun has risen not
only because I see it, but because by it I see everything else
– C.S. Lewis

T HIS IS THE hardest topic I had to write about, not because It's
the section where I have little thought on or little experience.
This is the hardest topic because it's been the biggest section of my
life. It is the area where I have experienced multiple highs and lows.
It's the section that I need to be careful with my words, for this is
the section I don't want the spotlight on me, but on the glory of God
or on why faith is so important. Faith? Something so simple yet so
big. People would define faith as the complete trust or confidence in
someone or something, in that higher being. Which makes sense. How
would I define faith and the importance in the notion, well it would
be that firstly, faith is something way more than just a complete trust
or confidence. Because sometimes confidence dies, confidence gets
broken. Faith to me is best described through the message version of
the bible.

*The fundamental fact of existence is that this trust in God, **is the firm
foundation under everything** that makes life worth living its our handle
on what we can't see. The act of faith is what distinguished our ancestors set
them above the crowd. (Hebrews 11:1-2)*

Faith is my foundation for everything. For who I am, my views on all areas and for what I align myself with, am I always right? Well no. I have failed, and I have questioned more times than I should, yet there is still a peace I feel and a hope that even the bottom of the barrel is not always the end. Truthfully it has been easier to hold on to faith when things are easy when life is going in the right direction, but it's when life is rough, when I am in the valley that to have hope or to hold on to my faith, and know that there is something bigger, that is what gets me through. I say 'usually' because there have been several moments in my life and in the last twelve months where I have drifted, and I have wondered why I went through the moment I have. Even now as I write this, there are many unanswered questions and many hurts that are still being mended. I have questioned tradition and tested areas where words have been spoken over me and about me. I have seen the many tangible and intangible objects that people swear their life to, whether it be substances they cannot live without, or to sporting, community organizations that they feel belonging to even to people, they put on that stage. I have seen faith, tested and I have seen unshakable faith in the moment when all the world has lost hope, when one is staring death in the face, to stand firm and hold onto the faith over all doctors all reports, look to small red words and feel victory and power in them.

I grew up believing that everything we do has a consequence and like I said my faith is the foundation for all actions committed, it has been somewhat easy to know or be exposed to faith, but with such ease to exposure it has also been hard to figure it out exactly what it means to myself, and not just something that I am told. One thing I have learnt is that there is a difference between faith and hope. One may hope in the times of sorrow and during the times of hardship, hope for the light at the end of the tunnel, but faith is the **rooted expectation** that there will be good that comes from the bad. It is the expectation that is steeped in the heart and in the spirit.

In the last year, I have come to learn there are two positions on the outlook to life, there are those who look merely at the logic of actions and need to know the reasoning behind life's why. Then there are those who defy reason and logic and lean on faith. Craziness or foolishness to lean on such a bold concept like faith, but there is an admiration in that as well. How I wish now that I could be one of those people. I have my faith but I have moments when I have doubted it and I have learned more towards logic and reasoning, where I crumble and fall at the hardships of life when I know better. Sometimes so transfixed on the problems that arise, faith is so small. Yet that's the beauty of it, that at the end of the day despite how small our faith is, if we hold on to it, we can move mountains, we can change the story around. I have seen that some moments in life that only through faith was impossible made possible. If you haven't figured out, I like the concept of life being a journey, when it comes to my Christian journey well that is one heck of a trek, but I am where I am now by taking that leap of faith. Simply put there is this inner understanding that my life would fail to have reason if I didn't have my faith, it would not be clear.

Someone once asked, why do I believe in God when he has put me through such hard things in life at such a young age. My response was because he never left. Yes, I have been put through some hard trials in life, everyone goes through hardship, but the thing is even when I failed to see it; God truly never left. God never gave me more than I could handle, despite screaming to the heavens and saying that I have had enough, God provided the means, he provided the way and its because of the courage and his grace that I can easily and boldly say that His promise never fails. He never left me, if anything I have failed many times and many times I left or moved away from him. You see faith to me is not a list of things I need to do, things I cannot do, because if it was well, I would never get it done and the list would become something I hate.

No, faith is that personal level, a connection. My faith and my journey will never be the same to others, but my faith is something I will keep with me for future generations of my family, which is seen through my family already, I have seen my grandmother pray for her family each morning before she starts the day, I have seen my parents pray for our family every morning and every night. One day last year as I was on holiday in the Philippines, my uncle sat me and my nieces down and we started talking on the family history, but the one thing

I learnt and took away from that conversation was how the faith of my grandmother, my uncles is being passed down to us the next generation.

He said, our prayers to God was so that you the next generation of De Guia, will live in the mercy and blessings of God and the faithful prayers of us. That made me think of the generations that come from faith, how whole families can turn and change the cycle through faith. There is a beautiful picture of linage that comes from the fact that faith and praying, goes beyond just us and now but its paving the way for our future generations.

Overall, I have learnt I cannot sum up faith, it is something you experience on your own. What I can leave with is that I have lived through moments of feeling locked up in deep darkness, where I have given up on life, and forgotten the good in life. Moments where I have said 'this is it, I am done, God is a lost cause', but because of those moments, because of knowing the darkness and feeling so far from God, I have also learnt that Gods loyal love won't run out, his merciful love is created new each morning. I think the best story that I felt really moved by in the bible is Lamentations 3 (the message version) there is a line that says 'I'm sticking with God, I say it over and over He's all I've got left.'

Like CS Lewis, I believe not because I see the sun rise but because of the rising sun I see everything else. Through having this faith, through aligning myself in the security of Gods promises, I am able to see the good amongst the bad, I am able to see Gods power and glory in the simplest thing like the sunrise if you have never watched a sunrise I recommend you do. Not only is it a magnificent sight to watch, but there is truly something beautiful and magical. Its like the sun comes out to show glory on earth, it highlights the fact that even in the darkest moments, in areas where it feels so dark, light will still reach it. There will be areas where light and darkness mingle, moments when you feel both up and down but there is a beauty in the simplicity. Even to those who don't hold on to faith, there is a beauty in knowing each day the sun rise and it brings with it light, and the shadows of the night once again go to bed.

The following poems in this section, bring light to my journey and struggle along the lines of faith, in times when life was heavy and silence was all that was around, brought about the moments of waiting in hope, the realization that the worst is never the worst because God wont ever walk out and fail to return. The poems I hope reflect the journey that can come from sadness, that hat faith has helped discover purpose, it has been the weapon to trump stress, anxiety and fear, even when we have no reason to believe that things will get better its through faith that our situations do in fact do improve. Overall like the rising sun, faith is that light that will always guide you through the darkness. I hope that is what is shown or felt through the following poems.

FAITH

THE PITTS & INNER PEACE

She was dying, all lost hope
Specialists to nurses, no answer they could find.
But day by day she blessed your name and smiled.
Report found in you; Your promise she held to.
'By your stripes I am healed'
By your stripes SHE was healed
Not in the way we saw,
Not in the method we hoped.
But in the means for your glory to be told.
for all saw the peace you provided,
all saw the faith and grace you gave.
Darkness and doubt surrounded,
yet she looked above and saw beauty in it all.
She saw the role you made her play.
You're words the light during darkness and fear.
Six months to live, 15 years, the end was set,
Many walked away, just let time pass accepted
Human limitations, you stayed faithful,
Never to leave never to forsake,
you stepped in your glory above all others.
Your plans not yet known. Three more years.
A promise in the waiting. Faith like none other.
flesh was weak, spirit her strength,
to live each day for the wonder of your presence.
became her declaration of promise, her cry for life.
Heartache and fear came up from time to time,
She did not curse, she did not hate,
Draw closer to you that's what she did?
till the sun crept through the 15th of that
forgotten month, a smile and praise, all known
she was home, she finished the race.
Even I still don't know, that lesson of faith
here I am in the depth of my sorrow, asking
why was she gone after so long of fighting.
A hope to look life through the faith she did.

For I live through the Holy spirit,
in Christ I am set free, no hold of fear on me,
just call out to God, draw close to him
see his power in the simple sunrise.
aching or breaking, lonely and lost
He hears all tears, he hears all trouble
No darkness too dark, his light still shines.
Orchestrating each section of my daily life
No matter what comes, I know that I am
Loved, through him who died, I am found.
I owe it to him all that I do, I am
who I am for who he showed himself to be.
He steps in whenever I am weak,
I stumble and fall but he picks me right up.
I can go through the valets and rest assured
He is with me, his rod and grace comfort me.
A beauty to dwell with God by myside.
Through the moment od doubt, may arise
and shout, you voice of truth, softly speaks.
What more can I say than thank you my king.

KELLY DE GUIA

When I say I am a believer, it does not mean
my life is grand, or everything is sorted out.
When I say I am a believer
I acknowledge all the highs and lows,
The moments I feel so far away,
and question the point in continuing.
I struggle with the fight of faith,
for there are still moments of despair
and prayer feels like empty words,
Sunday church just random songs,
and preaching pass through ear and ear
When I say I am a believer, it's no confirmation
I am screaming out the reminder more than declaring
This is who I am, for I'm lost more times than I'm found,
Only survived through the belief in my faith.
When I say I am a believer, its letting go and
Knowing God knows What he is doing,
his plans over mine, time is in his hands.
When I say I am a believer,
there's a hope that speaks to my soul.
Despite the valleys and the darkness,
I have seen the beauty in His grace,
I have felt the joy in Gods own embrace
When I say I am a believer, I'm confessing
I am a sinner. That I need God more then he
needs me, When I say I am a believer, I am
Screaming forgive me, over and over again.
till redemption fully felt and live, maybe
only till my dying day, will I stop saying
forgive me father, for I have sinned.
When I say I am a believer, I am telling
God, he is all I want, Him about the rest.
When I say I am a believer, its on my knees
Bearing all, not standing tall with pride.
For many times, I have failed and stumbled and fall

He still picks me up he still says I love you,
At times it's in the silence and in the confusion
God shows the way; shows the truth.
When I say I am a believer, I am saying
I need help and hope He hears my cries
I have faith to stick to him, despite the timing
He knows perfection in a way none other.
When I say I am a believer, I'm saying
There's no other way than Jesus.

In the darkest of times, in the depth of despair.
When all around is broken and bent,
there's a hope that sits in my soul.
A peace my faith will only know.
That despite the giants that stand
and taunt or the laughter in my face
from ones I thought knew what was
best the spirit says, be still and know
I am God. Though the waves may soar
and fire may burn, with him by side
I will not drown, embraced by him I will not burn.
So, shout with praise, shout it out loud
Jesus my savior, all glory to your name
What they see as failure, you've
Shown the way, a new beginning,
Found in your glorious grace.
Never alone in the sorrow, in joy the world will
See and know, only by your name,
am I where I am today.
I was broken and you picked up the pieces,
I was lost and you lit the way,
Amazing grace, a sweetness comes
In hearing your name, like the soft whisper
Amongst the breeze, you know the way
To speak right into my heart.

God, I need you more than you need me
a transformation starting from within.
Change me from the inside Lord,
a new heart is all I want. You are a God
of new beginnings, wash away the sin
from yesterday. For you alone are mighty.
You alone deserve all glory. Let your
light shine when all else fades. May
voices of distraction be silence by your praise.
A desperation like no other, Jesus I need you.
more than words can truly say, My lord
transform me from the inside out.
May I come to the river and be washed in your blood,
my sin be forgiven by the power of his love.
Remove all dirt spiritual and physical.
I plead my clear conscious to God above.
Every burden ever scar, be washed by your blood,
Come and join me, lets praise the God above.
It does not matter who are where you are
Jesus our savior, we cry we need you
in this very moment.

God your love is amazing, devoted and precious
Like a vow that is tested, or a fine ring of gold.
It endures overall, nothing to break or bend.
Faithful you have shown and faithful you always will be,
despite my failure, you stay forever.
Through the winter ache or the unknown
Beyond the mountains and horizons,
Your grace never too far.
For only your mercy is new daily, your love is the
the same never changing, from the brokenness
of the past to the hope and joy of tomorrow
To God be the glory, for you are might to save.
What more can I give but day after day
Shout loud your praise, with hands held high,
I will lift your name on high, for may my uttered words
bring glory to your name, for there is none like you.
May your presence be what known from the actions of
my life to the words that overflow, you're promise still
stands, great is your faithfulness despite all the heartache
you make a way, and still call my name.
You've held me when I was lost, you are father to the orphans
and heal the brokenhearted. You took me out from
the shadows of the shadows of the past, what was lost
now made found, what once was broken in you now made
whole. From the ashes of yesterday you bring about the beauty
of today, you washed away my shame and freed me from my guilt
I walk around each day, known to you by name, before I spoke
Your praise, you called me by name. What glorious grace
When you gave yourself for me, brought sin to the cross and
Carried it away. That's why I'll sing your praise each day,
to say thank you for who you are and what you've done for me

oh, what a gift, when I gave my life to thee
that you died for the sinner like me
your gracious gift, broke down the hardened walls
my savior, my father, forever my friend.
My guiding light, my inner peace,
What once was lost in you now found.
Oh, what serenity, the reckless love you gave for me
To take that sin and bear it hung upon the sinner cross.
Poked at and laughed about, the judgement you bore,
The guilt and shame meant for me, now on your
Shoulders when you took it from me.
To cut down the curtain and put sin in its place
You screamed Abba, my father.
Forgiveness let out, rumbled and shook,
Death could not hold you down, oh death
Now where is your sting, for the king of kings
Has broken the chains, resurrected king now
Seated in all his majesty, still loving and caring for me.
Despite the times of failure, where I stubbornly walked away.
you stand there arms open wide, waiting each day,
holding on to your promise, for what you have starred
you surely will finish, forgive me father, when I turn away
felt in the pits but comfort in your shade,
Your mercy remains and new day by day.
So, I'll spend all my days,
Singing glory to your name
For the precious blood of Jesus,
Covered sin and washed shame away.

You are Alpha and Omega, beginning and the end.
Jesus, the Savior, forever my friend.
In the valley of the low or the mountain on the high
Promise Forever you'll by my side.
The thoughts of the world, they trick, and they lie
little red words speak truth amidst the lies.
I hold onto hope, to stick by your side,
that's all I've got, in the darkest of times.
Both failure and praise nailed to the cross that darken day.
I may at times feel like the ground, pounded into mud.
Yet Your mercies new day by day. You show me repeatedly;
You're waiting to draw near.
I lay it all down, past present and unknown.
In you I am sure eternity secured.
You're Alpha and Omega. You're Abba, our father.
Living waters overflow. No fraught, no thirst always full.
You never walk out or fail to return. A promise to finish all you start.
Goodness and mercy come from up above.
All nations bow, all tongues confess only you are king over all earth.
You turned water to wine, gave sight to the blind.
Our bondage broken by the name we lift high.
In every season in every hour Jesus be known to all the earth.
I lay it down, surrender all to you, just guide me now, let me listen to you.
I'll go where you want, to the ends of the earth your name will be lifted,
by the whisper of comfort or the shout of praise,
all will know Jesus you are the way.
So Holy Spirit fill our souls, Holy Spirit break down our walls.
Bondage broken, all hearts are healed,
Jesus the savior defeated the deaths sting.
From the grave to the heavens, you put sin in its place.
No sting on me to fear no more, forever at peace Gods by my side.
For You're Alpha and Omega. The beginning and the end.
Jesus my savior, king forever my friend.

I was running from my past, hiding from tomorrow.
crying everyday hoping screams that's echoed
would reach the stars above.
To have felt lost and so confused, identity still unsure
Who am I supposed to be? What am I supposed to do.
For I have seen trouble, and I have seen pain.
Walked into darkness holding the hand of another,
They broke my bones and left me all alone.
Locked up in the darkness, like a corpse
inside a coffin. Did I screw it all up, will I ever get back out.
I cry out and plead for help, do you hear my prayers?
But it's the moment of my darkest hour confused and lost
is how I feel, I lay it down, I say I've had enough Jesus
Show me the way. Just like a child needing
The guidance from their father. You called me by my name,
said my child I'll always be here. I'm always there.
For when I felt like I hit rock bottom the only thing left
was the reminder of God above. The grip on hope
to pull me through. For you promised back in the day,
and you promise it today, tomorrow I'll remember it
Your loyal love, won't run out,
compassion won't dry out. In you
I find my refuge; in you I find my hope.
Each morning the sun shall rise, your mercies are
new day by day. So, I'll sing it in praise, I'll shout
It out loud. Each Day I'm sticking with God.
over and over, he is all I've got left.
Tomorrow will not be heavy but when life will feel
like the storm above. I'll go off and wonder by myself,
I'll enter silence and bow in prayer. To just wait and know
hope will always appear. No longer will I run from trouble.
No longer will I hide in the face of fear.
For my God is for me, who could be against me.

KELLY DE GUIA

WORDS ABOUT HER

A short and sweet written piece by one of the people that the words I have written so many poems and stories for. He was the sadness and beauty during a period of my life. My dear friend, Mr. Benjamin Glitsos.

I HAVE KNOWN KELLY only in the last year of the decade that she has been writing and working on this specific collection. That being said, only in the last year of knowing her have I seen firsthand how much she has changed and grown as a person and as a writer. In the last year I have been very (very, very etc.) honored to have watched her grow and have in some small way helped inspire her to do some of the most amazing things in that past twelve months, which includes this project, the publishing of 'Sadness and Beauty' as a book.

The way that Kelly thinks is always a fascinating topic for me; because I can tell and I hope you too have been able to see, especially by reading her poems, that it is so different from my own or most people's way of thinking. Kelly offers a differing perspective and stance on emotions and on simple moments and experiences. I directly asked her today: 'how do your emotions work', and she replied, that while some people compartmentalize their emotions, her emotions flow all through her and are intertwine. That where people at times find it difficult to express emotions, hers can clash and overflow. I think that's the beauty in her perspective, that though Kelly has and will have the moments of darkness that are her valleys, that despite her experiences of deep thought that she has and will go through, she has always been able to fully appreciate the beauty of a simple, sentimental moment. Kelly sees the balance beam in the good and bad in the moments that people often glaze over. It are the moments of daily activities or experiences like watching a sunset, something so simply that so easily just flows right through her whole being. The interplay of her thoughts and feelings produces a richness of experience that only some poets know. From reading this collection of hers, we are thankfully, able to have a slight insight into that rare outlook of life and the ability to experience some of the beauty and sadness she has lived through by the means of written words.

Lastly, I'm honored but mainly shocked to have given her the idea for the title of the book, that came about half a year beforehand, maybe around July 2018, the idea which came about during a moment when I actually made her quite annoyed during a car ride home. I had said that I think people's internal lives can be plotted onto two axes: excitement and fear versus beauty and sadness. *'I'm excitement and fear, and your beauty and sadness'* I said, surprised that there was no reply and that she in fact suddenly got quiet and left the car very quickly. Unaware of the impact then, I did not notice her brusqueness but after a few month, when we were talking, and this moment was brought back up in discussion she explained the quietness of that specific moment. She told me that she was annoyed because it reflected on her a bit too deeply. Now knowing Sadness and Beauty became a metaphor for the balance beam that she sees in all things love, life and her faith. Kelly girl, I'm glad to have known you so well then.

- Benji Boy.

GRATITUDE

Thanksgiving & Praise

THOUGH THESE ARE my words, the poems truly belong to the people they were written for. It does not matter, if they were the people who showed me the meaning of hurt and pain or the people who encouraged and taught me to never stop writing. It is through these individuals that I learnt to never stop expressing myself through the medium of words. The words are for all of them. Unknown to them, just how much of an impact their part in my life has had. It is through such people and their bond during certain seasons that helped made a moment of confusion clear and periods of heartache soon became trials of hope. It was the repeated lines that came up in my head daydreaming or jotted down words on post it notes during times of study and work, they became the words that helped express suppressed emotions. I am grateful for what I experienced because of them.

To my family, the De Guia tribe, thank you for the support. They say you can tell a lot about a person by their name I am grateful our name means 'The Guide' for you all have been my guide, my compass, my northern star. I know that whenever I am lost, De Guia will always lead me home. Thank you to my beautiful and talented niece, Patricia Balmocena who helped create such beautiful edits to show the artistic side to the concept of sadness and beauty in the three areas Love, Life and Faith, you my dear are amazingly talented. My family in the Philippines, thank you that you have shown how strong the bond of family can be. To my uncles you are the pillars of our family name I have learnt from all three of you, one I learnt that whatever happens

God has everything in control so there but to just smile at each day and count our blessings, one I have learnt that even if we look so tough, we all still need help and its okay to ask for help and to love unconditionally because that is a blessing in life and one I have learnt that we can always turn our lives around that we are not bound by the history of our name, that we are capable of achieving so much in life and that family will always be the source of joy and hope. My parents, Mom and Dad, thank you for the constant encouragement, and the guidance in every season, thank you for reminding me I can do everything I set my mind to, this book is evidence of your parenting. That you were always there always the greatest support. Thank you for the patience and the life lessons I will take with me. Thank you dad for teaching me the joy in reading and in storytelling. I am forever grateful to be known as your junior.

Keziah, Kylie and James, you are the best siblings God has blessed me with. Kez even though you're no longer here with me, I wrote because you saw the potential in me, I wrote because you were the first loss. I felt the intertwined notion of sadness in beauty the day you went away. I love you forever, and forever you will be remembered. Kylie and James, I owe it to both of you for sitting there and listening to me talk, where reciting lines of poetry over and over again became something you both wanted to hear (at times) and the thing, you knew was my specialty, even though you hated the constant question of asking if this made sense and debates over grammar, but you both have showed me that there is nothing stronger than the bond of siblings, despite our differences and our clashes you both have been there for me in everything. I am who I am because of what you my family have installed in me.

To the one who basically helped in penning the name of the book; you have been my sunshine, my box of tissues and also my reason behind the tears and my real-life version of George the Giraffe. Thank you is not even enough. but Benj I do want to say thank you. You saw what I could be way before I did, this book is because one night you spoke the words and it became a revelation to the balance beam of life. I'm forever grateful that you appeared and came into my life when you did. Loving the art of poetry just as much as I do, was the cherry on top when we met. I will always remember our shocked and pleased faces when we figured this out about each other. Thank you for re-igniting the reason behind why I write the night you invited me to that poetry event where I was watching you read and thought, I can do this again, thank you for letting the words once again flow. Thank you that you have always been supportive of my writing and life goals. It's funny how it only takes one person to come in and be the catalyst to unleash all hidden goals and be that push where self – doubt was somewhat strong. All I can say is thank you for being that person to me. It is because of all these people and especially you, that I have loved the words and I have hated the words, but now in this moment I know I have made them proud.

Lastly, every good gift comes from above, my writing though may have started out as an escape, now became my gift from God, I do everything in life so that others see him in me. Thank you to my heavenly Father, I have seen in my life the truth in your promise that you will never leave me nor forsake me, that I am where I am supposed to be in life. All things are possible through you, So, to God be the Glory. Forever and ever. Amen.

With all my words,
K.

CPSIA information can be obtained
at www.ICGtesting.com
Printed in the USA
BVHW081135290819
557143BV00001B/251/P